The A

Interest in Chinese objects displayed in my New England childhood home along with my mother's gifting me Mandarin lessons on vinyl records spurred an early fascination with the Chinese language. One of these items appears on the cover of this book, a 1929 lunar calendar from Fujian province.

While a Chinese major at the University of Massachusetts, I participated in a year abroad program at Tunghai University in Taiwan. One year was not enough and I decided to stay for two, despite reluctant acquiescence from UMass. Even with two years of study, I knew my language skills were insufficient. After demonstrating Mandarin language proficiency, I was accepted into the MBA program at National Chengchi University in Taiwan. I was thrilled, as I could not imagine anything better than attending graduate school with second language immersion. Three years of study and writing my thesis in Chinese bolstered my fluency.

Forty-seven years of learning Mandarin, a penchant for poetry in both languages, and time during a pandemic led to this volume.

Jonathan J. Babcock 2020

Chinese Poetry in Rhyme

Human and Computer Translation

中詩押韻英譯
人腦比電腦

Jonathan J. Babcock

白宗傑

Chinese Poetry in Rhyme:
Human and Computer Translation

Published by Jonathan J Babcock
Webster, Massachusetts USA
jonathanjaybabcock@gmail.com

Cover graphics by May Babcock, artist and paper maker
may@paperslurry.com

Thanks to Deborah Wade for everything.

Library of Congress Control Number: 2020919989

ISBN 978-1-7327759-2-3   paperback
ISBN 978-1-7327759-3-0   ebook

Works by Jonathan J Babcock

Boston to India 1858: Ship Journal of Joseph Manning Smith Jr.
Jonathan Babcock- Editor 2018
ISBN 978-1-7327759-1-6 paperback
ISBN 978-1-7327759-0-9 ebook

Zhu Tai Mei ji guan li ren yuan ling dao xing wei zhi yan jiu
住台美籍管理人员领导行為之研究
(Study of American Managers in Taiwan Leadership Behavior)
Jonathan Jay Babcock (Pai Tsung-chieh). 1981 (in Chinese)
LC Classification HD38.25.T28 B33 1981
LCCN 81216442 - out of print

Introduction

學如逆水舟 "Learning is a boat traveling upstream." During my four decade journey learning Chinese I was struck by the wide variety and quality of poetry translations from Chinese into English. Especially notable is lack of rhyme scheme in translated works. A joy of appreciating original Chinese poetry is the sound of its metered rhyme. When poems have three rhyming lines, English renditions often fail to reflect it. Instead, translations employ limited rhymes, or are free-form with no rhyme at all. Here, I sought to preserve the rhyming nature of Chinese verse and offer translations true to the writer's original feeling, imagery and sound.

Without rhyme, poetry loses its lyrical nature. My English translations of poems in this book all have rhyme. Most adhere to the original line rhyme scheme, such as AABA, or ABAB. In some poems, I have been fortunate enough to keep the original Chinese phonic rhyming sound.

Poems printed in traditional Chinese characters appear with an English computer translation below. On the following page, standing alone, is my translation. Computer translation is presented as a caution against using machine renditions for anything beyond short, direct, unambiguous prose.

Computers have ushered in a new dimension of translation. Machine language employs ones and zeros to assign graphics of letters in sequence to display human language.

Human sentences are often flawed grammatically. Despite these flaws, intended meaning is conveyed via context of subject matter and a reader's understanding of the world. Human speech is not one word, one definition, one exact set of grammatical rules meant to please artificial intelligence of machines, but revels in the beauty of turning a phrase.

Computer translations can be effective for words that hold one exact definition and for sentences adhering to common sentence patterns. Computer algorithms do not distinguish whether writing is poetry or prose, comic book or international treaty.

With three versions of each poem presented, bi-lingual and English-only readers can make meaningful comparisons. Notable errors in computer translations include incorrect choice of a word's multiple definitions. In "Sought Hermit Unfound", the original contains the characters 松下 "beneath pine". Instead of rendering original meaning, the computer proffered the Japanese brand name Panasonic.

Computers fail to recognize creativity. When machines have not previously cataloged creative phrases, all words except one or two are omitted. Inadequacies in relating colloquialisms are found. In "Autumn Thoughts", machine translation literally renders "people who break their intestines" instead of the English idea of a broken heart.

In many results, verb-object relationship is wrong. In "Home for a Memorial Day", a literal translation becomes "ask the winehouse" instead of the poetic line meaning, "where is there an inn?" Much time can be spent discovering the reasons for errors of computer translation.

Translation apps are a fantastic tool if used with awareness of their shortcomings with tailored restraint. If you invite a friend to "swing by later", an app may produce "以后摇摆." A phrase literally meaning "Swing later." Be wary.

Finally, please enjoy my translations by reading them aloud as a conveyance of living words written long ago reflecting timeless human emotion.

Contents

Life's Years Reach Not One Hundred 生年不滿百 2

A Flower Then Not 花非花 4

Da Lin Temple Peach Blossoms 大林寺桃花 6

Invite to a Friend 問劉十九 8

In the Rear Palace Chamber 後宮詞 10

Night Snow 夜雪 12

River Evening Song 暮江吟 14

Studying Lao Zi 讀老子 16

Official Granary Rats 官倉鼠 18

Meeting a Capital Envoy 逢入京使 20

Poem of Ones 一字詩 22

Autumn Eve 秋夕 24

Home for a Memorial Day 清明 26

Qin Huai River Mooring 泊秦淮 28

Written New Year's Eve 除夜作 30

Snow in Spring 春雪 32

Ode to the Willow 詠柳 34

Returning Home 回鄉偶書 36

Sought Hermit Unfound 尋隱者不遇 38

Drinking Alone Beneath the Moon 月下獨酌 40

Listening to a Zither 聽箏 42

Crossing the River Han 渡漢江 44

Spring Lyric 春詞 46

Autumn Lyric 秋詞 48

Listening to a Dulcimer 聽彈琴 50

Cold River Snow 寒江雪 52

Self Admonition 自遣 54

Autumn Thoughts 天淨沙 秋思 56

Spring Sleep 春曉 58

Journeysome Son 游子吟 60

While Drinking Wine 飲酒 62

Colorful Clouds 染雲 64

Farewell to my Daughter at Yin 別鄞女 66

Random Rhymes (1) 即事二首 68

Random Rhymes (2) 即事二首 70

South Bank 南浦 72

While Docked at Guazhou 泊船瓜洲 74

In the Mountains 山中 76

Soldier at Liang Zhou 涼州詞 78

New Bride 新嫁娘 80

A Painting 畫 82

Bamboo Retreat 竹里館 84

Deer Woodland 鹿柴 86

Ninth Month and Day Remembering My Brothers
九月九日憶山東兄弟 88

Ascending Stork Tower 登鸛雀楼 90

Sent to My Friend this Autumn Night 秋夜寄邱员外 92

Moss 苔 94

Limestone Rhyme 石灰吟 96

Passing by Chrysanthemum Pavilion 過菊江亭 98

For My Wife 贈内人 100

Docked Overnight at Maple Bridge 楓橋夜泊 102

Remembering
The courage that my mother had
–Edna St. Vincent Millay

and gratitude to
Cheng Ch'ing Mao 鄭清茂
University of Massachusetts Professor Emeritus
who introduced me to Chinese poetry so long ago

Poetry

詩

生年不滿百

生年不滿百, 常懷千歲憂
晝短苦夜長, 何不秉燭游
為了當及时, 何能待來茲
愚者愛惜费, 但为后世嗤
仙人王子橋, 難可與等期

無名 (25-220)

Less than a Hundred Years Old

Born less than a hundred years old,
often a thousand years of worry.
The days and the bitter nights are long,
why not swim by candlelight.
For the timely,
how can you stay to come to the z.
A fool cherishes a fee,
but sneers at the future.
Fairy Prince Joe,
difficult to be able to wait with.

Computer translation

Life's Years Reach Not One Hundred

Life's years reach not one hundred,
yet harbor all mankind's woes
Days are short, bitter nights long,
why not cavorting go?
Pleasure is of this moment,
why wait what future brings?
Fools love parsimony,
heirs later laugh and chortle
Despite the tale of Wangzi Qiao,
you'll ne'er be sage immortal

Anonymous (25-220)

花非花

花非花霧非霧
夜半來天明去
來如春夢幾多時
去似朝雲無覓處

Flowers are not Flowers

Flowers are not misty.
It's going to dawn at half the night.
Come like a spring dream is not many hours.
Go as if there is no place for the clouds.

Computer translation

A Flower then Not

A flower then not, a foggy mist not long
Here at midnight, fled by dawn
Like fleeting spring dreams
As morning clouds gone

Bai Ju Yi (772–846)

大林寺桃花

人間四月芳菲盡
山寺桃花始盛開
長恨春歸無覓處
不知轉入此中來

白居易 (772-846)

Da Lin Temple Peach Flower

April in the world is full of.
The peach blossoms of the mountain temple are in full bloom.
Long hates spring to return to nowhere to find.
I don't know how to get in here

Computer translation

Da Lin Temple Peach Blossoms

We live where April flowers seem all gone by
But mountain temple peach blossoms now come alive
So melancholy when our spring scene ends
Unaware the season moves so high

Bai Ju Yi (772–846)

問劉十九

綠螘新醅酒
紅泥小火爐
晚來天欲雪
能飲一杯無

白居易 (772-846)

Ask Liu Nineteen

Green 螘 new wine.
Small furnace of red mud.
It's snowy late.
Can drink a cup without

Computer translation

Invite to a Friend

Bubbling hue of a fresh wine lot
Warming in a small, red clay pot
It grows late, the sky bodes snow
Can you drink a cup, ...or not?

Bai Ju Yi (772-846)

後宮詞

淚濕羅巾夢不成
夜深前殿按歌聲
紅顏未老恩先斷
斜倚薰籠坐到明

白居易 (772-846)

Back Palace Words

Tears wet wipe dream can not be.
The front hall of the night was singing.
Red-faced old en first break.
Reclining smoked cage sat in the ming

Computer translation

9

In the Rear Palace Chamber

Tear-soaked silk scarf, dreams are gone
Late into the night the palace sounds of song
Her blush young countenance dropped from favor
Hunched towards the perfume censer she sits 'til dawn

Bai Ju Yi (772-846)

夜雪

已訝衾枕冷
復見窗戶明
夜深知雪重
時聞折竹聲

白居易 (772-846)

Night Snow

Has been surprised to sleep cold.
See the window clear again.
The night knew how heavy the snow was.
When you smell the sound of bamboo

Computer translation

Night Snow

I gasp from the chill of pillow and down
Then glance to window's papered glim
In dead of night, ware of snow's heavy crown
When hearing random, snapping, bamboo sounds

Bai Ju Yi (772-846)

暮江吟

一道殘陽鋪水中
半江瑟瑟半江紅
可憐九月初三夜
露似真珠月似弓

白居易 (772-846)

Twilight

A residual sun was in the water.
Half-Jiang Cersei half river red.
Pity the three nights of early September.
Exposed like a true pearl moon like a bow

Computer translation

13

River Evening Song

A waning sun's beam o'er the water spreads
Half the river rippled, the other red
What a third of September eve it is
Dew like pearls, crescent moon o'er head

Bai Ju Yi (772-846)

讀老子

言者不如知者默
此語吾聞于老君
若道老君是知者
緣何自著五千文

白居易 (772-846)

Read Laozi

The speaker is not as silent as the confidante.
This phrase is heard in lao jun.
If the old man is the knowledge.
Why comes from five thousand

Computer translation

Studying Lao Zi

"Preacher's words fail as the wise stay mum"
This adage I heard from this Esteemed One
If Daoist Lao Zi is indeed a sage
Why was his lengthy tome ever done ?

Bai Ju Yi (772–846)

官倉鼠

官倉老鼠大如斗
見人開門亦不走
健兒無糧百姓饑
誰遣朝朝入君口

曹鄴 (816-875)

Official Hamster

The official barn mouse is as big as a fight.
See people open the door also do not go.
The children are hungry without food.

Computer translation

17

Official Granary Rats

Official Granary rats large as baskets
Doors open, people seen, none even scatter
Soldiers rationed, populace starving
Who allows these gentlemen their daily larder?

Cao Ye (816-875)

逢入京使

故園東望路漫漫
雙袖龍鍾淚不幹
馬上相逢無紙筆
憑君傳語報平安

岑參 (715-770)

When You Enter Beijing You Make a Visit to Beijing

The east of the park is long.
The double-sleeve dragon bell was silent.
Meet the paperless pen right away.
Be safe with the word "jun."

Computer translation

19

Meeting a Capital Envoy

Home is a long arduous road leading east
Welling tears over-dampen both of my sleeves
A chance meeting on horseback with no paper or brush
Passing words of good tiding depends now on thee

Cen Shen (715-770)

一字詩

一帆一槳一漁舟
一個漁翁一釣鈎
一俯一仰一場笑
一江明月一江秋

陳沆 (1785–1826)

A Word of Poetry

Sails and a boat.
A fisherman a hook.
One pitch and one laugh.
One Jiangming moon, one river autumn

Computer translation

Poem of Ones

One sail, one oar, one fishing skiff
One fisherman, one hook to fish
One cast, one strike, one mirthful scene
One river moon, one autumn stream

Chen Hang (1785-1826)

秋夕

銀燭秋光冷畫屏
輕羅小扇撲流螢
天階夜色涼如水
臥看牽牛織女星

杜牧 (803–852)

Autumn Night

Silver candle autumn light cold picture screen.
Light small fan pounce.
The sky is as cool as water.
Sit back and watch the cow-drawn actress

Computer translation

Autumn Eve

Silver candle and autumn pale, stark on a painted screen
Her delicate silk fan, flits at a firefly's gleam
In the palace, shades of night oh so watery cold
Watching Altair and Vega, lovers star-crossed as she

Du Mu (803-852)

清明

清明時節雨紛紛
路上行人欲斷魂
借問酒家何處有
牧童遙指杏花村

杜牧 (803-852)

Qingming

During the Qingming season, there was rain,
Pedestrians on the road want to break their souls.
Ask the winehouse where it is,
Pastoral children refer to the apricot flower village

Computer translation

Home for a Memorial Day

Grave Sweeping Day in the rain and mist
The road-weary traveler seeks some rest
Asking a herd boy where is an inn
Apricot Blossom Village and waves far ahead

Du Mu (803-852)

泊秦淮

煙籠寒水月籠沙
夜泊秦淮近酒家
商女不知亡國恨
隔江猶唱後庭花

杜牧 (803-852)

Po Qinhuai

Smoke cage cold water moon cage sand.
Night park Qin Huai near the wine house.
Businesswoman does not know the death of the country hate.
Across the river juju sings the back court flower

Computer translation

27

Qin Huai River Mooring

Mist shrouds chill water, moon covers a sand spur
Qin Huai River night docking, with a tavern near
Ladies of the night, unawares of the nation's plight
At the riverside still sing, *Jardin de Fleur*

Du Mu (803-852)

除夜作

旅館寒燈獨不眠
客心何事轉淒然
故鄉今夜思千里
霜鬢明朝又一年

高適 (701–765)

Except for the Night Work

The hotel's cold lights are alone.
The guest heart turned poignant.
Hometown tonight think a thousand miles.
Frost ming Dynasty another year

Computer translation

29

Written New Years Eve

By an inn's spartan lamp so isolate sans sleep
Each thought in the heart renders rue so deep
Tonight longing home o'er thousand miles away
Frosted beard as the morrow another year doth see

Gao Shi (701–765)

春雪

新年都未有芳華
二月初驚見草芽
白雪卻嫌春色晚
故穿庭樹作飛花

韩愈 (768–824)

Spring Snow

There is no Fanghua in the New Year.
The grass sprouts were startled at the beginning of February.
Snow is late for spring.
So wear the tree as a flying flower.

Computer translation

Snow in Spring

No fragrant blooms at New Year's time
Shoots of grass are next month's surprise
White snow sneers at spring colors late
'Til garden is dressed by flora full a-fly

Han Yu (768-824)

詠柳

碧玉妝成一樹高
萬條垂下綠絲縧
不知細葉誰裁出
二月春風似剪刀

賀知章 (659-744)

Willow

Jade makeup into a tree high.
Ten thousand of the green silks that fall.
I don't know who made the fine leaves.
February spring breeze like scissors

Computer translation

Ode to the Willow

Jade, jade adorns the tree's ascent
Countless pendants of green silk braids
Who has patterned each delicate leaf?
Shears of mid-spring's shaping wind

He Zhi Zhang (659-744)

34

回鄉偶書

少小離家老大回
鄉音無改鬢毛衰
兒童相見不相識
笑問客從何處來

Home Town Books

Little and young leave home.
The village sound has no change in the hair decay.
Children don't meet each other.
Laugh and ask the guest where he came from.

Computer translation

35

Returning Home

Youthful I left home, now aged to stay
Local accent unchanged, hair thinning gray
Young friends greet, but neither recognize
Smile to ask this visitor, are you from far away?

Ho Zhi Zhang (659-744)

尋隱者不遇

松下問童子
言師採藥去
只在此山中
雲深不知處

賈島 (779—843)

The Seeker Doesn't Meet

Panasonic asked the boy.
The teacher took the medicine.
Only in this mountain.
The clouds are deep lying

Computer translation

37

Sought Hermit Unfound

To a boy beneath a pine I seek
Master's picking herbs he speaks
On this mountain close by here
Clouds so thick I know not where

Jia Dao (779—843)

月下獨酌

花間一壺酒，獨酌無相親
舉杯邀明月，對影成三人
月既不解飲，影徒隨我身
暫伴月將影，行樂須及春
我歌月徘徊，我舞影零亂
醒時同交歡，醉後各分散
永結無情遊，相期邈雲漢

李白 (701-762)

Ms. Shimo-Germany

A pot of wine in the flower room,
with no love.
Raise a glass to invite the moon,
to the shadow into three people.
The moon does not drink,
the shadows follow me.
Temporary companion moon will be shadow,
line music and spring.
I sing the moon wandering,
I dance chaos.
Wake up and meet,
get drunk and scatter.
Forever knot ruthless lying,
phase-phase Yunhan

Computer translation

39

Drinking Alone Beneath the Moon

A flask of wine in the flower garden,
drinking alone ne'er a friend to meet
Raising my cup to toast the moon,
I see my shadow making us three
The moon fails at drinking,
as my shadow with me hovers
I play with moon and shadow,
before brief spring is over
Moon keeps a beat to my singing,
my shadow freely sways
When awake we keep good company,
post drunk we drift away
Yet our ties will ever bind
and shall meet in the Milky Way

Li Bai (701–762)

聽箏

鳴箏金粟柱
素手玉房前
欲得周郎顧
時時誤拂絃

李端 (738-786)

Listen to the Zither

Songzheng gold column.
In front of the jade room.
Want Zhou Lang Gu.
It's a time to brush the strings by mistake

Computer translation

41

Listening to a Zither

From the zither's gilded bridge melodies arise
Perfect hands upon the ornate instrument ring
Seeking to attract a suitor's eyes
She randomly plays an errant string

Li Duan (738-786)

渡漢江

嶺外音書絕
經冬復歷春
近鄉情更怯
不敢問來人

李頻 (818-876)

Cross the Han River

The sound of ing book is absolutely overwhelming.
After winter and spring.
The near-home feeling is more timid.
Dare not ask the people

Computer translation

43

Crossing the River Han

No tales or letters over the mountains here
All winter and now through spring
Nearing home my mood waxes fear
Afraid to ask news from those passing

Li Pin (818-876)

春詞

新妝宜麵下朱樓
深鎖春光一院愁
行到中庭數花朵
蜻蜓飛上玉搔頭

劉禹錫 (772-842)

Spring Words

New makeup should be lower than Zhulou.
Deep lock spring light a hospital sad.
line to the atrium to count the flowers
The dragonfly flew on the jade dagger

Computer translation

Spring Lyric

Stepping out a red-chamber, beauty's face freshly made
Locked here alone with spring, sullen, dismayed
Walking the main garden, counting budded flowers
A dragonfly alights, on her hairstick of jade

Liu Yu Xi (772-842)

*red-chamber: female living quarters

秋詞

自古逢秋悲寂寥
我言秋日勝春朝
晴空一鶴排雲上
便引詩情到碧霄

劉禹錫 (772-842)

Autumn Words

Since ancient times, there has been a quiet fall.
I say autumn is better than the Spring Dynasty.
The sky is on the clouds.
Then the poem is introduced to the blue

Computer translation

47

Autumn Lyric

Autumn's arrival forever sad and forlorn
But I say fall, surpasses a spring morn
Line of cranes upon billows in the fair sky
Emotive poetry to an azure-jade heaven is born

Liu Yu Xi (772-842)

聽彈琴

泠泠七弦上
靜聽松風寒
古調雖自愛
今人多不彈

Listen to the Piano

On the seven strings.
Listen quietly to the cold.
The ancient tone is self-love.
Today's people do not play

Computer translation

Listening to a Dulcimer

Pling pling on the seven-string
Listening to *Pine Winds*, taking it in
Though I love this old melody
Folks today, fail to play thee

Liu Zhang Qing (714-790)

寒江雪

千山鳥飛絕
萬徑人踪滅
孤舟蓑笠翁
獨釣寒江雪

柳宗元 (773-819)

Cold River Snow

Thousands of mountain birds fly out.
The trail of people is gone.
Lonely boat.
Alone fishing for the cold river snow.

Computer translation

Cold River Snow

A thousand hills no birds on the wing
Ten thousand paths no footprints cling
A straw-cloaked old man in a solitary boat
Fishing alone the river's snowy sting

Liu Zong Yuan (773-819)

自遣

得即高歌失即休
多愁多恨亦悠悠
今朝有酒今朝醉
明日愁來明日愁

羅隱 (833-910)

Self Dispatch

It's time to go off the song.
It's sad and hateful.
In this dynasty there is wine and drinking.
Tomorrow's sorrow comes tomorrow

Computer translation

Self Admonition

In success I loudly sing, indifferent when I fail
Much sadness and regret, creates depression's veil
If wine be had in morning, then imbibed I will be
Let the tomorrow's trouble be tomorrow's travail

Luo Yin (833-910)

天淨沙 秋思

枯藤老樹昏鴉
小橋流水人家
古道西風瘦馬
夕陽西下
斷腸人在天涯

馬致遠 (1260-1364)

Tian Sha Qiu Si

The old old vine is a crow.
Little Bridge water people.
Gudao West wind thin horse.
Sunset.
The people who break their intestines are at the end of the
earth.

Computer translation

55

Autumn Thoughts

Withered vines on an old tree at dusk with roosting crows
A small bridge over flowing water near someone's home
On an old byway in autumn's breeze stands a thinning roan
Late day sun settling towards the sky's westward dome
A heart-rent traveler so far away to roam

Ma Zhi Yuan (1260-1364)

春曉

春眠不覺曉
處處聞啼鳥
夜來風雨聲
花落知多少

孟浩然 (689–740)

Chun Xiao

Spring sleep is not aware of.
Smell the birds everywhere.
The wind and rain came in the night.
How much flowers are lost.

Computer translation

Spring Sleep

Dawn was lost in deep spring sleep
Songbirds fill my ears so sweet
Night sounded wind and rain
Countless petals fell unseen

Meng Hao Ran (689-740)

游子吟

慈母手中線
遊子身上衣
臨行密密縫
意恐遲遲歸
誰言寸草心
報得三春暉

The Wanderers Chanted

Mother hand line.
The tourist is dressed.
Close to the line.
I'm afraid of being slow to come back.
Who speaks with a grass heart?
It was reported for three spring.

Computer translation

Journeysome Son

Loving mother thread in hand
Son's journeying coat a-darning
Fine so fine last stitches fly
Fretting long long returning
Pray tell, how this scion's heart
E'er honor her springtime nurture?

Meng Jiao (751-814)

飲酒

結廬在人境，而無車馬喧
問君何能爾？心遠地自偏
採菊東籬下，悠然見南山
山氣日夕佳，飛鳥相與還
此中有真意，欲辨已忘言

陶淵明 (365-427)

Drinking

Knotted in a human situation,
and no horse noisy.
Ask Jun Honor?
The heart is far from self-biased.
Under the east fence of chrysanthemum,
see the south mountain.
The mountain is good day by day
and the birds are with each other.
There is a true meaning here,
want to distinguish has forgotten

Computer translation

While Drinking Wine

I built a hut in the village here
Yet no noise of cart or horse appear
One may ask how can that be?
My mind can wander earthly free
At the eastern fence picking mums low
My eyes lift and the southern hills show
At sundown mountain air refreshes so
As paired birds aloft return to home
In this scene truth's truth I find
Yet words to describe it flee my mind

Tao Yuan Ming (365-427)

染雲

染雲為柳葉
剪水作梨花
不是春風巧
何緣見歲華

王安石 (1021-1086)

Dyed Clouds

Dye the clouds are willow leaves.
Cut the water for pear blossoms.
It's not a spring breeze.
Why see the old Hua

Computer translation

Colorful Clouds

Colorful clouds to willow leaves
Clear water to blossoming pears
If spring breeze workings fail us
What shall bring the lush new year

Wang An Shi (1021-1086)

別鄞女

行年三十已衰翁
滿眼憂傷只自攻
今夜扁舟來訣汝
死生從此各西東

王安石 (1021-1086)

Don't Be a Girl

The Chinese New Year's Eve of the line has fallen.
Full eyes of sadness only self-attack.
Tonight the flat boat came to the trick.
From then on to the west and east

Computer translation

Farewell to My Daughter at Yin

A broken man at thirty years
Slings of pain, eyes brimming tears
Tonight a boat, her final crossing
Dead and living, forever parted

Wang An Shi (1021-1086)

即事二首

雲從鐘山起
卻入鐘山去
借問山中人
雲今在何處

王安石 (1021–1086)

That's Two Songs

Clouds start from Zhongshan.
But go into Zhongshan.
Ask the people of the mountains.
Where is the cloud today?

Computer translation

Random Rhymes (1)

Clouds from Mount Zhong rise
Yet may in the same subside
Ask for me of dwellers there
Where now the clouds reside

Wang An Shi (1021–1086)

即事二首

雲從無心來
還向無心去
莫覓无心处
無心無處尋

王安石 (1021-1086)

That's Two Songs

Clouds never come.
Also to the mindless to go.
No more than a heartless place.
Nowhere to look.

Computer translation

69

Random Rhymes (2)

Clouds form without volition
Then vanish lacking intention
Ne'er seek the inanimate center
It's essence defies location

Wang An Shi (1021-1086)

南浦

南浦随花去
迴舟路已迷
暗香無覓處
日落畫橋西

王安石 (1021-1086)

Nanpu

Nanpu goes with the flowers.
The boat road is lost.
There is no place for dark incense.
Sunset Paint Bridge West

Computer translation

South Bank

Along the south bank drifting with blooms
Boat's homeward course now dim
Everywhere hidden floral perfume
West setting sun painted bridge

Wang An Shi (1021-1086)

泊船瓜洲

京口瓜洲一水間
鍾山隻隔數重山
春風又綠江南岸
明月何時照我還

王安石 (1021-1086)

Boat Guazhou

A water between Jingkou Guzhou,
Zhongshan is only a few heavy mountains apart.
The spring breeze and the south bank of the Green River,
When will the moon take my back.

Computer translation

73

While Docked at Guazhou

Jingkou and Guazhou a river divides
Here to home in Mount Zhong a few hills to pass by
Spring breezes again green the river's southern side
O how long 'til moonlight be my homeward guide?

Wang An Shi (1021–1086)

山中

長江悲已滯
萬里念將歸
況屬高風晚
山山黃葉飛

王勃 (650-676)

In the Mountains

The Yangtze River is already in tatafter.
Miles will come home.
It's a high wind late.
The yellow leaves of the mountains fly

Computer translation

In the Mountains

Yangtze River and I now sullen and listless
Yearning to return countless miles distant
Alpine winds too, signal autumn is nigh
In mountain upon mountain yellowed leaves fly

Wang Bo (650–676)

涼州詞

葡萄美酒夜光杯
欲飲琵琶馬上催
醉臥沙場君莫笑
古來征戰幾人回

王翰 (687–726)

Cool State Word

Wine night light cup.
If you want to drink the slug immediately urged.
Drunk lying in the sand junmo laughs.
Ancient came to fight several people back

Computer translation

Soldier at Liang Zhou

Fine vintage wine in a cup of translucent jade
Drink and lute song insatiable 'til the horseman's call is played
Ne'er mock if drunk on the battlefield I lie
For how many return from all history's campaigns?

Wang Han (687-726)

新嫁娘

三日入廚下
洗手作羹湯
未諳姑食性
先遣小姑嚐

王建 (768-835)

New Bride

Three days into the kitchen.
Wash your hands for soup.
No agus.
Advance the little aunt to taste

Computer translation

New Bride

Married three days in the kitchen to cook
First wash my hands then make a soup
Mother-in-law's taste I'm still not clear
So first ask my young sister-in-law to try a scoop

Wang Jian (768-835)

畫

遠看山有色
近聽水無聲
春去花還在
人來鳥不驚

王维 (701-761)

Draw

Look at the mountains far and colored.
Near listening to the water silent.
Spring to flowers are still there.
People come to bird is not surprised

Computer translation

A Painting

Distant mountains' hue so clear
Water is silent, listen near
Spring passes, flowers still remain
People approach yet birds feel no fear

Wang Wei (701-761)

竹里館

獨坐幽篁裡
彈琴復長嘯
深林人不知
明月來相照

王維 (701-761)

Bamboo

Sit alone in the claustrophobic.
Play the piano and re-squeal.
Deep forest people do not know.
The moon will take a picture

Computer translation

Bamboo Retreat

Sitting alone in the bamboo grove dim
Strumming my zither loud I sing
Deep in the forest no one will know
Only the moon and the light it brings

Wang Wei (701-761)

鹿柴

空山不見人
但聞人語響
返景入深林
復照青苔上

王維 (701-761)

Deer Firewood

There is no one in the empty mountains.
But it's a voice.
Back into the deep forest.
Re-photographed on the moss

Computer translation

Deer Woodland

This spacious hill I see none around
But my ears hear talking sounds
Deep forest lets in shifting light
Illuminate o'er a moss-green crown

Wang Wei (701-761)

九月九日憶山東兄弟

獨在異鄉為異客
每逢佳節倍思親
遙知兄弟登高處
遍插茱萸少一人

王維 (701-761)

September Ninth,
the East Brothers of the Rembrance Mountain

Being alone in a foreign country is a foreign visitor.
Think of your relatives every holiday.
The distant brother ascended high.
There's one less person in the line

Computer translation

Ninth Month and Day Remembering My Brothers

Ever an outsider, never accepted in
Festival deepens thoughts for kin
Sensing my brothers highlands climb
Wearing dogwood sprays, less mine

Wang Wei (701-761)

登鸛雀樓

白日依山盡
黃河入海流
欲窮萬里目
更上一層樓

王之換 (688-742)

The Den

Day by day.
The Yellow River flows into the sea.
Want to be poor.
Better

Computer translation

Ascending Stork Tower

The sun sets near the mountains
Yellow River to the sea it runs
If an endless vista you desire
To one more flight do aspire

Wang Zhi Huan (688-742)

秋夜寄邱员外

怀君属秋夜
散步咏凉天
空山松子落
幽人应未眠

韦应物 (737-792)

Autumn Night Sent Qiu Outside

Waijun is an autumn night.
Take a walk in a cool day.
Empty mountain pines fall.
The scounl should be sleepless

Computer translation

Sent to My Friend this Autumn Night

Remembering my friend this autumn night fondly
Out in the cool air, strolling, humming softly
In the deserted mountain, a pine cone falls
You, a recluse, asleep, ought not be

Wei Ying Wu (737-792)

苔

白日不到處
青春恰自來
苔花如米小
也學牡丹開

袁牧 (1716-1797)

Moss

Day is not a place.
Youth comes right in place.
Moss flowers are as small as rice.
Also learn peony open

Computer translation

Moss

Sunlight not reaching where
Spring green dares appear
Moss buds small as rice
Yet bloom as a peony fair

Yuan Mu (1716-1797)

石灰吟

千錘萬鑿出深山
烈火焚燒若等閒
粉骨碎身渾不怕
要留清白在人間

于謙.(1398-1457)

Lime

Thousands of hammers chisel out of the mountains.
Fire and fire if idle.
The powder bone is not afraid.
To remain innocent in the world

Computer translation

Limestone Rhyme

Hammer chisel, hammer chisel, taking from mountains deep
Raging flame, kilned burned, mundane as can be
Bones to powder, body asunder, fully unafraid
Remain pure and innocent, despite the human reach

Yu Qian (1398–1457)

過菊江亭

杖履逍遥五柳旁
一辭獨擅晉文章
黃花本是無情物
也共先生晚節香

于謙 (1398–1457)

Over Jujiang Pavilion

The cane is on the side of the five willows.
A single word is a good article.
Yellow flowers are heartless.
Also Mr. Evening Festival fragrance

Computer translation

Passing by Chrysanthemum Pavilion

Ambling with my cane by Taoqian's* willow trees
Mastering books of Qin, every word I read
Wilted flowers were never sentimental things
Yet still lend fragrance to my waning eve

Yu Qian (1398-1457)

*Tao Yuan Ming (365-427)

贈內人

禁門宮樹月痕過
媚眼惟看宿鷺窠
斜拔玉釵燈影畔
剔開紅焰救飛蛾

張祜 (785-849)

Giver

The gated palace tree is marked by the moon.
The eye is only to see the nest of cebus.
Tilt-pulling jade lamp shadow.
Clear the red flame to save the moth

Computer translation

99

For My Wife

Upon gated palace trees, the moon traced overhead
Her enchanted eyes alone see a heron's nesting bed
Sliding out a jade hairstick by candle's shadowy light
She spares a flying moth, snuffing out the flame of red

Zhang Hu (785-849)

楓橋夜泊

月落烏啼霜滿天
江楓漁火對愁眠
姑蘇城外寒山寺
夜半鐘聲到客船

張繼 (circa 753)

Maple Bridge Night Berth

The moon falls in the dark and frosty.
Jiang Feng fishing fire to sleep.
Hanshan Temple outside The City of Gusu.
The night bell bell to the passenger ship.

Computer translation

Docked Overnight at Maple Bridge

Moon sets as crows call amid a frosted sky
River maples, fishing lamps stir a rueful sleepy time
From HanShan Temple beyond Suzhou city walls
Midnight tolling reaches the traveler's sampan side

Zhang Ji (circa 753)

Poem Index

A Flower Then Not 花非花...4

A Painting 畫...82

Ascending Stork Tower 登鸛雀楼...90

Autumn Eve 秋夕...24

Autumn Lyric 秋詞...48

Autumn Thoughts 天淨沙 秋思...56

Bamboo Retreat 竹里館...84

Cold River Snow 寒江雪...52

Colorful Clouds 染雲...64

Crossing the River Han 渡漢江...44

Da Lin Temple Peach Blossoms 大林寺桃花...6

Deer Woodland 鹿柴...86

Docked Overnight at Maple Bridge 楓橋夜泊...102

Drinking Alone Beneath the Moon 月下獨酌...40

Farewell to my Daughter at Yin 別鄞女...66

For My Wife 贈内人...10

Home for a Memorial Day 清明...26

In the Mountains 山中...76

In the Rear Palace Chamber 後宮詞...10

Invite to a Friend 問劉十九...8

Journeysome Son 游子吟...60

Life's Years Reach Not One Hundred 生年不滿百...2

Limestone Rhyme 石灰吟...96

Listening to a Dulcimer 聽彈琴...50

Listening to a Zither 聽箏...42

Meeting a Capital Envoy 逢入京使.................................20

Moss 苔..94

New Bride 新娘...80

Night Snow 夜雪...12

Ninth Month and Day Remembering My Brothers
九月九日憶山東兄弟...88

Ode to the Willow 詠柳..34

Official Granary Rats 官倉鼠..18

Passing by Chrysanthemum Pavilion 過菊江亭.................98

Poem of Ones 一字詩..22

Qin Huai River Mooring 泊秦淮......................................28

Random Rhymes (1)即事二首...68

Random Rhymes (2)即事二首...70

Returning Home 回鄉偶書..36

River Evening Song 暮江吟..14

Self Admonition 自遣..54

Sent to My Friend this Autumn Night 秋夜寄邱員外...........92

Snow in Spring 春雪...32

Soldier at Liang Zhou 涼州詞...78

Sought Hermit Unfound 尋隱者不遇.................................38

South Bank 南浦..72

Spring Lyric 春詞...46

Spring Sleep 春曉..58

Studying Lao Zi 讀老子...16

While Docked at Guazhou 泊船瓜洲.................................74

While Drinking Wine 飲酒..62

Written New Year's Eve 除夜作.......................................30